KILLER SHARKS, KILLER PEOPLE

by Victor Gentle and Janet Perry

Gareth Stevens Publishing
A WORLD ALMANAC EDUCATION GROUP COMPANY

Please visit our web site at: www.garethstevens.com
For a free color catalog describing Gareth Stevens' list of high-quality books and
multimedia programs, call 1-800-542-2595 (USA) or 1-800-461-9120 (Canada).
Gareth Stevens Publishing's Fax: (414) 332-3567.

Library of Congress Cataloging-in-Publication Data

Gentle, Victor.
    Killer sharks, killer people / by Victor Gentle and Janet Perry.
       p. cm. — (Sharks: an imagination library series)
    Includes bibliographical references and index.
    ISBN 0-8368-2826-7 (lib. bdg.)
    1. Shark attacks—Juvenile literature. [1. Shark attacks. 2. Shark fishing.]
    I. Perry, Janet, 1960- II. Title.
    QL638.93.G46 2001
    597.3'1566—dc21   00-052251

First published in 2001 by
Gareth Stevens Publishing
A World Almanac Education Group Company
330 West Olive Street, Suite 100
Milwaukee, WI 53212 USA

Text: Victor Gentle and Janet Perry
Page layout: Victor Gentle, Janet Perry, and Scott Krall
Cover design: Scott Krall
Series editor: Heidi Sjostrom
Picture Researcher: Diane Laska-Swanke

Photo credits: Cover, p. 17 © James D. Watt/Innerspace Visions; p. 5 © Ben Cropp/Innerspace Visions;
p. 7 Photofest; p. 9 © Ron & Valerie Taylor/Innerspace Visions; p. 11 © Jeff Rotman/Innerspace
Visions; p. 13 © Amos Nachoum/Innerspace Visions; p. 15 © Jerry Greenberg/Innerspace Visions;
p. 19 © Mark Strickland/Innerspace Visions; p. 21 © Marilyn Kazmers/Innerspace Visions

Printed in the United States of America

1 2 3 4 5 6 7 8 9 05 04 03 02 01

Front cover: A sand tiger shark swims off the coast
of North Carolina. The sand tiger is ranked fourth
in terms of the number of attacks on humans.

TABLE OF CONTENTS

Words that appear in the glossary are printed in **boldface**
type the first time they occur in the text.

A WICKED REPUTATION

Sharks have been known as killers for over twenty-five hundred years.

Ancient writings tell of shark attacks on humans as far back as 500 B.C. Explorer Ferdinand Magellan reported sharks eating people during his world voyage from 1519 to 1522. Brook Watson, who later became Lord Mayor of London, lost his leg to a shark in 1749, when he was just fourteen years old.

Other reports of sharks eating people have come down to us over the years. Only in the 1970s, however, did the shark really sink its teeth into the public's imagination. A certain book that was made into a movie did the trick.

These are the jaws of a tiger shark, the largest shark **species** that attacks people. Two much larger sharks, the whale shark and the basking shark, eat tiny plants and animals and don't attack humans.

JAWS

In 1974, *Jaws* burst onto the scene. *Jaws* is a horror story about a man-eating shark that terrorizes a seaside town in New England. The book was made into a movie. The book sold more than ten million copies, and the movie made hundreds of millions of dollars. The story made people think great white sharks killed people on purpose — and that's wrong.

"What I now know," says *Jaws* author Peter Benchley, "is that there is no such thing as a **rogue** shark which develops a taste for human flesh."

Even so, the great white shark (now officially called the "white shark") attacks more humans than any other shark species. That scares people! "How can we protect ourselves?" they demand.

This poster art was for *Jaws 3* (1983). The movie shark was 35 feet (10.7 meters) long — more than 12 feet (3.7 m) longer than any white shark scientists have found.

REDUCING THE RISK?

Many people have tried to make shark **repellents**. These don't work, but two protection devices do.

One good protection device is the anti-shark bag. Injured swimmers climb into the bag. The bag floats, but the bag's shape doesn't look tasty to sharks. Also, no blood or body fluids get out of the bag to tell sharks that something yummy is ready to eat.

Another device that seems to work well is the stainless steel suit. Underwater photographers and scientists Ron and Valerie Taylor made the suit to wear while diving to study sharks.

Common sense can protect you from sharks, too. It's good to avoid cloudy water, sparkling jewelry or fabrics, and water with dead animals or blood in it.

Here, Valerie Taylor tries out her stainless steel, chain mail suit with the help of a blue shark. She could only get the shark to bite by stuffing the arm with fish.

BAD, BUT NOT THE WORST

Blacktip, hammerhead, bull, and spinner sharks attack more people along North America's east coast than any other sharks. But in the past ten years, these four villains have managed to kill just one person among them.

Worldwide, sharks from each of five species (bulls, blacktips, hammerheads, tigers, and sand tigers) attack more people than do sharks of any other species — that is, any other except one. Add up the attacks by all five species. The total is still less than the number attacked by the "baddest" shark of them all.

The worst of these five species, the tiger shark, is the second most dangerous shark species in the world.

Do you know which is the most dangerous?

This sand tiger shark has a fearsome-looking set of jaws. It usually attacks people only when angered. It prefers to eat small fish, **rays**, other sharks, **crustaceans**, and **squid**.

THE MAIN MAN-EATER

White sharks attack and kill more people than any other shark species — but how many is that?

Along North America's west coast, most attacks on people are made by white sharks, and just a few by other species. But in the last seventy-five years, there have been only about ninety attacks by white sharks, and just eight deaths.

Worldwide, over the last hundred years, there have been roughly 70 to 100 attacks per year by all species. About seven to ten people have died from these attacks each year. White sharks caused just under half the deaths. More recently, in the last ten years, white sharks have accounted for only one out of every seven deaths.

A white shark goes for **bait** in the ocean off Australia. After *Jaws*, these sharks were hunted without mercy. Shark hunters got high prices for sets of jaws or teeth.

WHAT ARE THE CHANCES?

Your chances of being killed by a shark are very, very small. You stand a better chance of winning the lottery, being struck by lightning, or dying from a bee sting than being attacked and killed by a shark.

You will more likely die of an illness, being in a car accident, drowning, eating food with harmful germs, or being shot! About 1,000 times more people die every year from accidents with guns in the United States alone than from shark attacks worldwide.

Count all the people killed in all shark attacks. The total doesn't come close to the number of people who are killed by each other — or the number of sharks killed by people.

Underwater photographer Doug Perrine nurses a hand injury from a Caribbean reef shark. Divers working with sharks are among the people most likely to suffer attacks.

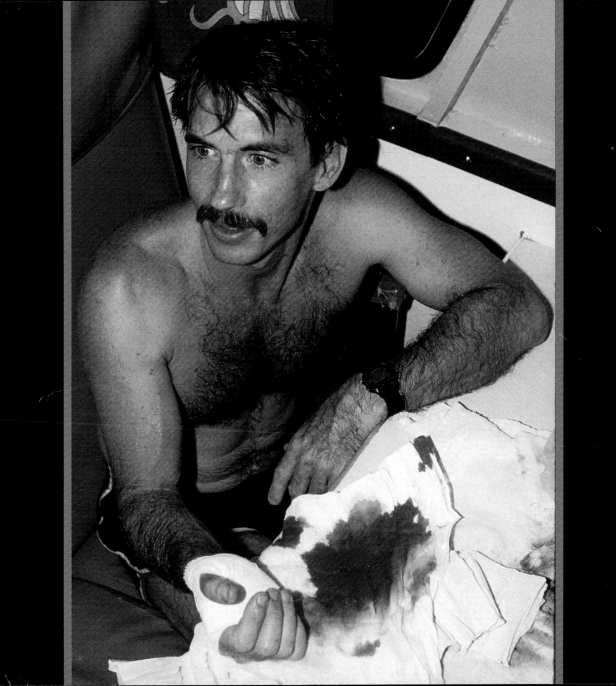

SHARK KILLING FUN

Some people who fish as a sport will hunt and kill sharks for the fun of it.

Recently, one U.S. shark fishing **tournament** alone killed more than two hundred blue sharks. There are hundreds of shark fishing tournaments every year in North America, Australia, Japan, South Africa, and elsewhere.

Often using speedboats and **sonar** for tracking the shark, sport fishers find, catch, and kill tens of thousands of sharks every year.

Sport fishers ride the ocean waves off Big Island, Hawaii, as they pull their prey — a mako shark — alongside their boat, using a **gaff** jammed through the mako's lower jaw.

SHARK KILLING BUSINESS

Commercial fishing kills enormous numbers of sharks every year — many more than are killed by sport fishing.

More than thirty million sharks are caught and killed on purpose, for their meat, their oil, or their skin, and sometimes just for their fins — for shark fin soup!

Even worse, scientists think that seventy million to a hundred million sharks are killed every year as **"bycatch."** That means that the commercial fishing ships do not try to catch and kill them. However, the sharks just get trapped in nets and lines that are meant to catch other fish.

A harmless zebra shark is caught in a net meant for other fish in the Andaman Sea to the south of Myanmar. Many millions of sharks die trapped as bycatch every year.

GOING, GOING...

Sharks killed fewer than a hundred humans in the past ten years. People have killed hundreds of millions of sharks during the same time period.

Sharks are not able to have babies quickly enough to keep up with the huge number of sharks that people kill — especially when pregnant sharks are often killed right along with the other sharks. Even before they are born, the babies inside don't have a chance.

In recent years, the huge increase in shark deaths is endangering many shark species.

"If the **carnage** continues," says shark scientist Sonny Gruber, "species that have lasted 400 million years could vanish within 50 to 100 years."

Fins are cut from blue sharks and mako sharks by fishers on the coast of Baja California, Mexico. Typically, the rest of the shark is wasted, often thrown back into the sea to die.

MORE TO READ AND VIEW

Books (Nonfiction) *Eugenie Clark: Adventures of a Shark Scientist.* Ellen R. Butts and
  Joyce R. Schwartz (Shoe String Press)
Eyewitness Activity File: Shark. Deni Bown (DK Publishing)
Informania Sharks. Informania (series). C. Maynard (Candlewick)
A Look Inside Sharks and Rays. Keith Banister (Reader's Digest)
Sharks (series). Victor Gentle and Janet Perry (Gareth Stevens)
Sharks: Voracious Hunters of the Sea. Secrets of the Animal World
  (series). Isidro Sánchez (Gareth Stevens)

Books (Fiction) *The Escape.* (*Animorphs #15*). K.A. Applegate (Scholastic)
Shark Bites: True Tales of Survival. Greg Ambrose (Island Bookshelf)
The Shark Callers. Eric Campbell (Harcourt Brace)
Terror Below!: True Shark Stories. All Aboard Reading (series).
  Dana del Prado (Grosset and Dunlap)

Videos (Nonfiction) *Great White Shark.* (20th Century Fox)
Shark Attack! (NOVA)
Shark Encounters. (National Geographic)

PLACES TO WRITE AND VISIT

Here are three places to contact for more information:

Greenpeace
702 H Street NW
Washington, DC 20001
USA
1-202-462-1177
www.greenpeace.org

World Wildlife Fund
1250 24th Street NW, Suite 500
Washington, DC 20037
USA
1-800-CALL-WWF
www.wwf.org

Vancouver Aquarium
P.O. Box 3232
Vancouver, BC
Canada V6B 3X8
1-604-659-3474

To find a zoo or aquarium to visit, check out **www.aza.org** and, on the American Zoo and
Aquarium's home page, look under <u>AZA Services</u>, and click on <u>Find a Zoo or Aquarium</u>.

WEB SITES

If you have your own computer and Internet access, great! If not, most libraries have Internet access. The Internet changes every day, and web sites come and go. We believe the sites we recommend here are likely to last, and that they give the best and most appropriate links for our readers to pursue their interest in sharks and their environment.

www.ajkids.com
This is the junior <u>Ask Jeeves</u> site — it's a great research tool. Some questions to try out in <u>Ask Jeeves Kids</u>:

> *What do sharks usually eat?*
> *Do sharks bite even when they're dead?*

You can also just type in words and phrases with "?" at the end, for example:

> *Shark repellents?*
> *Feeding frenzy?*

www.flmnh.ufl.edu/fish/sharks/statistics/ GAttack/mapusa.htm
Shark Attack Map of the USA. Look at the columns where the numbers are. Notice the places where attacks occur most often.

www.mbayaq.org/lc/kids_place/kidseq.asp
This is the Kids' E-quarium of the Monterey Bay Aquarium. Make postcards, print out coloring pages, play games, go on a virtual deep-sea dive, or find out about some marine science careers.

kids.discovery.com/KIDS
Click on the Live SharkCam. See a live leopard shark and live blacktip reef sharks!

oberon.educ.sfu.ca/splash/tank.htm
It's the Touch Tank. Click on a critter or a rock in the aquarium to see more about it.

www2.orbit.net.mt/sharkman/index.htm
Enter the Sharkman's World near Malta. He's a scuba diver who is completely soaked in anything even a little bit sharky. You'll find poetry, music, and shark pictures there. The Sharkman is not a scientist, but he loves to talk sharks with other shark people who love how cool sharks are — people like you!

www.pbs.org/wgbh/nova/sharks/world/ clickable.html
It's the Clickable Shark. Click on any part of the shark picture to find out how sharks work.

www.pbs.org/wgbh/nova/sharks/world/ whoswho.html
Here's a shark "family tree." Click on any of the titles, and you'll see what kinds of sharks belong in the same group, and why. If you see a picture of a shark you don't know, use the Shark-O-Matic to get answers.

GLOSSARY

You can find these words on the pages listed. Reading a word in a sentence helps you understand it even better.

bait (BATE) — food used to attract animals that people want to trap, catch, or kill 12

bycatch (BYE-kech) — sea creatures caught by accident in nets meant for other fish 18

carnage (KAR-nij) — much bloody killing 20

commercial (kom-ER-shul) — for business purposes; to sell 18

crustaceans (krus-TAE-shunz) — animals with hard outer shells like suits of armor 10

gaff — a large hook for holding big fish 16

rays (RAEZ) — shark-related fish with wide, flat bodies, winglike fins, and long tails 10

repellents (ree-PEL-ants) — substances to make things or animals move or stay away 8

rogue (ROHG) — out of control, rebellious 6

sonar (SOH-nar) — an instrument that bounces sound off underwater objects in order to find them 16

species (SPEE-shees) — a group of plants or animals that are like each other in many ways 4, 6, 20

squid (SKWID) — a sea creature with ten legs (or tentacles) coming from its head; squid can be smaller than an inch (2.5 cm) or larger than 60 feet (18.3 m) 10

tournament (TURN-a-ment) — a contest of skill where the winners often get prizes or money 16

INDEX